JUN 1 3

MICHAEL TOWNSEND'S

Where Do PRESIDENTS Come From?

AND OTHER PRESIDENTIAL STUFF OF SUPER-GREAT IMPORTANCE

DIAL BOOKS FOR YOUNG READERS
an imprint of Penguin Group (USA) Inc.

DIAL BOOKS FOR YOUNG READERS · A DIVISION OF PENGUIN YOUNG READERS GROUP
PUBLISHED BY THE PENGUIN GROUP
PENGUIN GROUP (USA) INC., 375 HUDSON STREET, NEW YORK, NY 10014, U.S.A.
PENGUIN GROUP (CANADA), 90 EGLINTON AVENUE EAST, SUITE 700, TORONTO,
ONTARIO, CANADA M4P 2Y3 (A DIVISION OF PEARSON PENGUIN CANADA INC.)
PENGUIN BOOKS LTD, 80 STRAND, LONDON WC2R ORL, ENGLAND
PENGUIN IRELAND, 25 ST. STEPHEN'S GREEN, DUBLIN 2, IRELAND (A DIVISION OF PENGUIN BOOKS LTD)
PENGUIN GROUP (AUSTRALIA), 250 CAMBERWELL ROAD, CAMBERWELL, VICTORIA 3124, AUSTRALIA
(A DIVISION OF PEARSON AUSTRALIA GROUP PTY LTD)
PENGUIN BOOKS INDIA PVT LTD, 11 COMMUNITY CENTRE, PANCHSHEEL PARK, NEW DELHI - 110 017, INDIA
PENGUIN GROUP (NZ), 67 APOLLO DRIVE, ROSEDALE, AUCKLAND 0632, NEW ZEALAND
(A DIVISION OF PEARSON NEW ZEALAND LTD)
PENGUIN BOOKS (SOUTH AFRICA) (PTY) LTD, 24 STURDEE AVENUE, ROSEBANK,
JOHANNESBURG 2196, SOUTH AFRICA
PENGUIN BOOKS LTD, REGISTERED OFFICES: 80 STRAND, LONDON WC2R ORL, ENGLAND

DESIGNED BY JASMIN RUBERO
TYPOGRAPHY BY MICHAEL TOWNSEND
TEXT SET IN CCBLAHBLAHBLAH
MANUFACTURED IN CHINA

1 3 5 7 9 10 8 6 4 2

LIBRARY OF CONGRESS CATALOGING-IN-PUBLICATION DATA
TOWNSEND, MICHAEL (MICHAEL JAY), DATE.
MICHAEL TOWNSEND'S WHERE DO PRESIDENTS COME FROM? : AND OTHER
PRESIDENTIAL STUFF OF SUPER-GREAT IMPORTANCE.
P. CM.
ISBN 978-0-8037-3748-8 (HARDCOVER)
1. PRESIDENTS—UNITED STATES—COMIC BOOKS, STRIPS, ETC.
2. PRESIDENTS—UNITED STATES—JUVENILE LITERATURE. 3. GRAPHIC NOVELS.
I. TITLE. II. TITLE: WHERE DO PRESIDENTS COME FROM?
E176.1.T74 2012
973.09'9—DC23
2012004103

Table of Contents

Some Pre-content Content

So, would you kids mind if I asked you a quick question?

GREAT! Okay, the question is, "What do you want to be when you grow up?"

When I grow up, I want to be a crazy robot who fights crime.

Perhaps you should learn a little about the job before you decide that it's what you want to be when you grow up...

I sure do! There are lots of great books out there!

WELL... I don't think a book like that would ever be made... Sorry.

AN INTRODUCTION

The purpose of this introduction is to help you (the reader) better understand what this book can do for you!!!

And, probably, the most amazing thing about this book is that it can help you learn all kinds of fascinating things about various presidential topics!

Now, let's take a quick look at what topics will be covered...

First, in chapter 1, we'll learn...

how the job of President got its start...

but to do this correctly, we need to take a moment to remember how the United States and its government got their start...

This chapter will quickly move through a very fascinating part of America's history, and I promise it will be more fun than a barrel of

Ninja Hamsters

Next, in chapter 2, we'll learn . . .
who the first President was . . .

and how he grew up to become a great leader who played a large role in shaping the job of commander in chief!

Plus, we'll learn a bunch of not so important stuff like . . .

He looked great on a horse . . .

he had a great throwing arm . . .

and he had horrible teeth!

This chapter is destined to be more fun than a barrel of

Angry Muffins

GRRRRRRR!

Then, in chapter 3, we'll take a look at...

a bunch of common (and not so common) questions about the presidential election process and then attempt to answer them ...

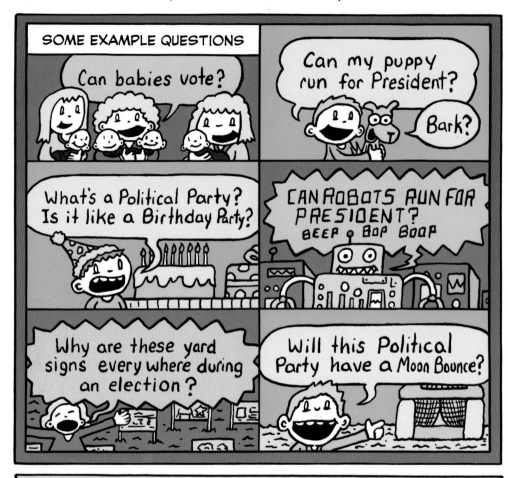

So, if you ever want to vote, or perhaps one day be President, then this chapter is for you... (Plus, it's guaranteed to be more fun than a barrel filled with itty-bitty tiny barrels!)

After that, in chapter 4, we'll learn...

all about the White House (the place where the President both lives and works).

This home is so full of interesting facts and important stories that if it were possible to turn each of those facts and stories into hamsters...America would be having a big hamster problem about now...

Lucky for us, interesting facts and important stories are not able to become hamsters, but they can be used to fill up our White House chapter, making it more fun than a pygmy hippo wearing a barrel.

In chapter 5, we'll...

spend some time taking a close look at different aspects of the President's actual job...

From the fun-filled perks and fulfilling work side of the job...

to the hidden dangers and daunting duties side of the job...

Plus, some interesting and weird stuff splashed here and there...

Finally, in chapter 6, we'll

take a quick look at what happens when a President becomes a...

FORMER PRESIDENT

Both these chapters are certain to be more fun than a barrel full of invisible skunks.

GROSS

STINKY

UGGG

Now that you have a brief idea of what each chapter
has to offer, it's time to strap on your reading gear...

make your way to your favorite reading place . . .

and get to learning!!!!!

HAVE FUN AND PLEASE READ SAFELY!

Chapter 1

Where Do Presidents Come From?

This chapter takes a look at how the United States and its Constitution came to be, because without them, there would be no President!

THE DECLARATION OF INDEPENDENCE

THE CONSTITUTION

First, let's travel WAAYYY back in time to the mid-1700s, when it was fashionable for men to powder their hair or wear wigs. A long time before awesome stuff like TVs, monster trucks, or even the U.S.A. existed yet.

It was also a time when two powerful nations, Great Britain and France, were constantly fighting with each other like cats and dogs.

Well, not exactly like cats and dogs; they fought like humans did in the mid-1700s (the point was they fought a lot)...

The mid-1700s was also a time when 13 British colonies (3,000 miles across the ocean from Great Britain) were thriving in the "New World." Since Great Britain was very busy with the French, the colonies were generally left to govern themselves . . .

But even though the colonists had developed very independent spirits, they still considered themselves to be proud British citizens!

As the British colonies flourished, they found themselves being confronted with a very British problem... their French neighbors!

Soon, the land disputes erupted into fighting.

When Great Britain found out about the problem, they borrowed lots of money and sent lots of troops to take charge of the fighting.

And so by 1758 the "French and Indian War" was officially under way. It was called this because American Indians had joined in on the fight. (Some tribes sided with the French, some the English.)

In 1763 the war came to an end. The results: Great Britain was the winner, so the French had to leave "New France." This made the 13 colonies very happy!!!

But over in Great Britain the happiness quickly faded when King George and the Parliament got a knock at the door...

To help pay off the war debt, the British Parliament and the king decided to impose a tax on various paper products in the colonies (it was called the Stamp Act). The colonists were not happy about the tax for many reasons...

The anger over the Stamp Act spread quickly throughout the colonies . . . (thanks to paper products).

This is Tyranny!

No Taxation without Representation

TYRANNY was quickly becoming the word of the day...

TODAY'S WORD OF THE DAY IS TYRANNY | Today's word... | sounds like | Tear·A·knee

SLIP OW

NOT Tear a Knee

Tyranny is a word that can describe an oppressive government that bullies its citizens and stomps on their natural rights, such as freedom of speech or religion.

In response to the Stamp Act, representatives from several different colonies got together to write out their complaints in a letter for the king (the gathering was called the Stamp Act Congress).

ANYONE ELSE HAVE ANYTHING TO ADD?

I DO! It's A PICTURE!

GET IT!

KING GEORGE IS A

TYRANNY-SAURUS

SORRY CRAZY BUNNY, THIS IS SUPPOSED TO BE A CIVIL LETTER FROM RESPECTABLE ENGLISHMEN

SIGH

Parliament responded to the letter by ending the Stamp Act, but it was a short-lived win because the king still intended to tax the colonies without their consent (just in new ways).

The king's next tax was an import tax on British goods such as tea, paint, glass, paper, and lead. The colonists responded by boycotting all taxed goods . . .

BRITISH GOODS ARE BAD! British Goods are Bad!

Tensions grew, and on March 5, 1770, a number of frightened British soldiers fired into an angry mob of colonists . . . killing several.

This event became known as the Boston Massacre and was reported widely. The colonists' anger grew. Thanks to the boycotts, Parliament ended all the import taxes except for the one on imported tea . . . proving that they still refused to grant the colonies a say in how they were taxed.

On Dec. 16, 1773, a large group went down to the Boston docks. Some of them were dressed as Mohawk Indians and they dumped all the unloaded tea into the harbor as an act of protest! This event became known as the "Boston Tea Party."

I heard we were dressing up, but nobody told me there was a theme...

The king and Parliament were furious about the events in Boston. They decided to make an example of the naughty Massachusetts colony.

First, they made all the colonists wear funny ugly hats . . .

JUST KIDDING

but they *did* shut down all local governments in Massachusetts . . .

and closed the port of Boston (among other mean things).

The harsh actions worried the other colonies, so in September 1774, they decided to send representatives to Philadelphia to meet and discuss what should be done.

The group was called "The First Continental Congress."

Once again, they decided to write out their complaints and demand that they should not be taxed without representation. Since it was still a civil letter, no mean drawings were sent . . .

They planned to meet again if things did not get better . . .

Things did not get better.

About six months after the first Continental Congress met, a Massachusetts militia clashed with British soldiers in the small village of Lexington (a short distance from Boston).

Which side fired the first shot is still open to debate, but it would later become famously known as "THE SHOT HEARD ROUND THE WORLD"!

A month later the Continental Congress met again. This time they decided to assume control of the militias and form a Continental Army, assigning it a commander (General Washington) and giving them a mission . . .

Believe it or not, there was still hope that Great Britain and the colonies would kiss and make up... but that hope was quickly fading.

During the winter of 1775-76, while the Continental Army was camped outside Boston, a pamphlet called *Common Sense*, by Thomas Paine, began to show up everywhere . . .

HMMM

COMMON SENSE By THOMAS PAINE

Common Sense was an easy to understand essay on why the colonies should declare themselves independent from Great Britain . . .

It was a hot seller, like bananas at a monkey convention.

BANANA STAND

The fever for independence was catching. Rhode Island and Virginia would be the first to declare themselves independent states!

Soon after that, on July 4, 1776, the Congress officially declared that all the colonies were independent states by signing a document called the Declaration of Independence.

Now, all its signers and those who joined the fight were officially traitors to the crown . . .

Leave some room for the rest of us, John Hancock!

A crime punishable by DEATH!!!

The 13 states had wanted a say in how they were governed and now they had it! But their old government wasn't about to let them go without a difficult fight, and from the beginning the odds were stacked against them...

For example, Great Britain had the biggest, baddest navy around...

The states really didn't have a navy (at least at the start of the war).

QUACK QUACK QUACK QUACK

Great Britain's army was professional, well-trained, and experienced . . .

The states' army was...well...a work in progress...

WELL, AT LEAST WE DON'T LOOK LIKE LOBSTERS!

Plus, in addition to their regular troops, the king had hired Hessian troops to help with the fight.

Hessians were German soldiers, famous for their nastiness!

The states did not have any Hessians . . .

I HEAR THEY HAVE HORNS UNDER THOSE HELMETS!

YOU MEAN THEY'RE MAN-I-CORNS?

GASP

It's no wonder King George thought winning the war would be as easy as stealing candy from a baby.

HMMM...

YOINK

HA HA HA

But he was in for a surprise.

SLAP

So, here's what happened: A very, very quick overview of

AMERICA'S WAR FOR INDEPENDENCE!

Also known as the Revolutionary War (in just two pages).

As the fighting began...

BOOM

BANG

The Americans realized that one of their biggest challenges would be to survive to fight another day (not necessarily to win major battles).

Through good times and bad (they were mostly bad) they managed to fight on. Mastering the art of midnight escapes didn't hurt!

GENERAL, WE HAVE THE REBELS CORNERED!

GOOD, WE'LL CRUSH THEM IN THE MORNING.

THUMP CRUNCH

SHHH!

tiptoe, men, tiptoe...

GASP GENERAL, THEY'RE GONE!

JUMPING PENGUIN BABIES!

They learned to make small wins go a long, looooooong way...

REMEMBER THAT TIME ABOUT SIX LOSSES AGO WHEN WE WON A BATTLE?

I SURE DO! THAT WAS AWESOME!

They also managed to hold the army together even though soldiers were rarely paid, or provided with adequate food or clothing... (this was especially a problem during the cold winters).

HEY, WHERE ARE YOUR SHOES?

THEY WORE OFF!

I ATE MINE...

Their love of freedom kept them going, and every day they survived was another day that Great Britain had to pay for an expensive war 3,000 miles away from home...

When the French saw that the 13 independent states had the ability to stay in the fight, they decided to openly assist them with troops, a navy, and money!!!

By 1781, after the Americans had defeated the British at the Battle of Yorktown, the British finally gave up!!!

So, after the war the United States consisted of 13 individual governments that, during the war, had united together under a document called the Articles of Confederation . . .

The document was an agreement that the states would work together for some basic common stuff like defense . . .

After the war there were some leaders who desired a slightly stronger central/federal government than what currently existed. They had many reasons for wanting this. Here are a few examples:

But there were also some political leaders who disliked the idea of giving a federal/central government more power. They had many reasons too. Here are just a few:

Both sides of the issue had good points, but how would they figure out what to do? They decided to do what they always did when faced with difficult questions...

LET'S GO ASK THE MAGICAL BEAR WHO LIVES IN THE AMERICAN WOODS!

Oh, Magical Bear, what should we do?

HMMM...

Just kidding, they did not do that, but some leaders did call for a meeting to address the "Articles" problem. Their true intentions of wanting to write a brand-new Constitution would be revealed at the meeting.

What's a constitution?

A constitution is a written document that lays out the rules and principles for a government to follow...

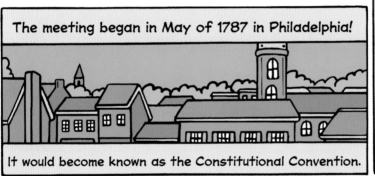

The meeting began in May of 1787 in Philadelphia!

It would become known as the Constitutional Convention.

Once the secret goal of the meeting was revealed, the debate began. Many different plans of what the new government should look like were put forth, then there were debates and compromises ...

PLAN A
NO, PLAN B
PLAN C...

IDEAS ...

#@¢#!

DEBATES ...

HOORAY FOR PLAN ABC

COMPROMISES ...

The final result was a new Constitution that carefully laid out a blueprint for a federal government that would be divided into three branches. Each branch was given very specific and distinct powers.

THE LEGISLATIVE BRANCH	THE EXECUTIVE BRANCH	THE JUDICIAL BRANCH
Made up of the Congress	Consists of the President and Vice President	Made up of Federal Judges . . .
This branch is the law-making part of the federal government.	This branch is in charge of enforcing the law and it is headed by the President.	This branch is made up of courts and judges that deal with federal law.

One reason for making 3 branches was to divide the power, hopefully making it harder for the government to become a tyrannical mess!

HA HA HA HA HA HA BOW DOWN TO YOUR LEADER, MY FUNNY HAT PEOPLE!

AND THAT IS WHERE THE PRESIDENCY COMES FROM!

SO, THE PRESIDENT ISN'T ALL-POWERFUL?

NOPE, BUT IT'S STILL A VERY IMPORTANT JOB.

SIGH

And now let's take a closer look at the three branches.

THE LEGISLATIVE BRANCH

ALSO KNOWN AS: THE UNITED STATES CONGRESS

It's the law-making branch and it's divided into two parts . . .

THE SENATE and the HOUSE OF REPRESENTATIVES

- Each state gets two senators
- They serve six-year terms
- The people elect their senators (it wasn't always this way)
- Currently there are 100 senators

- The number of representatives a state gets is based on population
- They serve a two-year term
- The people elect their representatives
- Currently there are 435 representatives

QUESTION: CAN THIS BRANCH MAKE ANY OLD LAW THEY WANT?

Such as...
LAW: Any time you see a turtle, you must sing it a LOVE SONG!

Oh, Turtles are Awesome, so much cooler than Opposums! I Love you, I Love you!

GRRA

ANSWER: NOPE...

Article One of the Constitution lays out a very limited list of what kinds of laws the legislative branch can create. (This includes creating and maintaining an army and navy, coining money, and regulating foreign affairs and trade.) All powers not listed are left for the states themselves.

THE EXECUTIVE BRANCH

This branch is headed by the President of the United States (the P.O.T.U.S.) and the Vice President of the United States.

THE PRESIDENT

THE VICE PRESIDENT

They both serve four-year terms.

The President is both . . .

RIIIP

The head of state and . . .

RIIIP

The commander in chief of the armed forces.

His or her job is to enforce the laws of the land and to preserve, protect, and defend the Constitution. Executive departments can be created by Congress to help the President enforce the law. The President can appoint the department heads, but the Senate must approve the choice!

So, how is the President elected?

By a process called the Electoral College.

What's that?

We'll cover that in chapter 3.

Grrrrr Fine

And we'll learn more specifics about this job in chapter 5.

A CLOSER LOOK AT... THE JUDICIAL BRANCH

The judicial branch is the home to the "Highest Court in the Land," the Supreme Court.

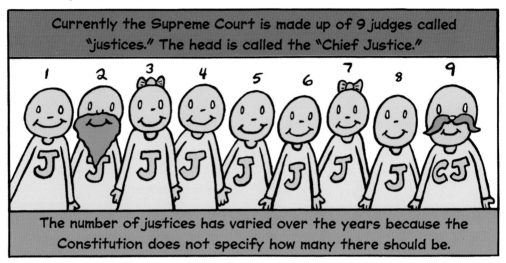

Currently the Supreme Court is made up of 9 judges called "justices." The head is called the "Chief Justice."

The number of justices has varied over the years because the Constitution does not specify how many there should be.

Supreme Court justices are appointed by the President but must be approved by the Senate. Once they are approved, their terms are for life or until . . .

They lose their minds...

LOOK! A UNICORN! A UNICORN!

They retire...

I'm getting too old for this...

They are fired (impeached) for bad behavior...

STOP THIEF!

Or they die!

ARGGG!

SPLAT

The Constitution also allows for other lower federal courts to be created if Congress feels the need (they did feel the need!).

Now that we have a very basic idea of what's in the Constitution, it's important to note that it could only become the law of the land if 9 states would ratify it . . .

Eventually, by 1788, enough states gave their consent and the Constitution became official. It would be two more years until all the states ratified the Constitution, though.

One last important thing to mention before we bring this chapter to a close is that in 1791 the "Bill of Rights" was officially added to the Constitution . . .

WHAT IS THE BILL OF RIGHTS?

The Bill of Rights is (more or less) a list of rights that the government can NOT take away from its citizens . . .

Like, freedom of speech . . . (even speech against the government)

and the right to bear arms . . . (this is not what was meant).

The U.S. Government smells like feet!

No . . . that's you . . .

Hey, I have rights! Gimme!

BEAR ARMS

WHAT IS A CONSTITUTIONAL AMENDMENT?

A Constitutional Amendment is a change or addition to the Constitution. The men who wrote it (the framers) made sure that adding amendments was possible but also a very difficult process that required a lot of work and consent . . .

AMENDMENT PROCESS
1. Proposal
Ⓐ Ⓑ
Ⓒ Monkey
2. RATIFY Proposal
Ⓐ

BLAH BLAH BLAH

The framers knew that if they made the Constitution too easy to amend, then tyranny could quickly result.

Let's end by summarizing what we've learned so far...

We've learned how the United States became the United States...

Tyranny led to anger and protest, then uniting and fighting and winning.

Next, we learned about the creation of the United States Government.

We also learned that the framers of the Constitution divided up the power of the federal government into 3 separate branches.

And let's not forget that most of the people in politics are accountable to the voters...

The only thing we haven't covered yet is who would become the first President of the United States. Shockingly, the diverse and independent citizens of the U.S.A. seemed to all be in agreement on who that person should be...

Curious who this George is? Then turn to the next chapter!

(If you've found a lot of this chapter interesting, then go to your local library, get some books, and learn more! If you need help finding books, just ask a magic bear (or your librarian) for some help!)

Chapter 2

Who Was the First President of the United States?

This chapter looks at the life of George Washington and the many reasons he is super-important.

George was born into a pretty well-to-do family (not poor, not super-rich). He was his mom's first child (she would have several more) but not his dad's (he already had some kids from his first wife, who had died).

Obviously, the reason we can be sure he would not say these things is that neither the United States nor video games existed yet . . . What we do know is that George wanted to be just like his two older half brothers.

Since both his half brothers went to England to get fancy educations, George wanted this too . . . (A fancy education helped one to better fit into High Society.)

HAS A FANCY EDUCATION

WHAT A GENTLEMAN

DOES NOT

When George was eleven, his father died.

This meant that money would be tight and George, being the oldest left at home, would need to stay and help care for his younger siblings . . . George did his best to learn what he could while stuck at home. He even copied down every line of a book called . . .

THE RULES OF CIVILITY AND DECENT BEHAVIOR

THE BOOK WAS FILLED WITH 110 RULES TO FOLLOW TO BE A BETTER GENTLEMAN, SUCH AS:

RULE 9: Do not spit into a fire when with company.

RULE 107: Do not speak with your mouth full . . .

THEN I SAID . . .

At 16 George was excited to get a job as a surveyor.

WHAT'S A SURVEYOR?

A surveyor is somebody who, with the help of math and special measuring tools, maps out land. Back then there was a lot of land in need of mapping . . .

It wasn't an easy job. The frontier could be a very wild and dangerous place, but the job did pay well!

DANGEROUS ANIMALS

DANGEROUS TERRAIN

DANGEROUS WEATHER

As George gained more knowledge about land, he began to buy property. He was also growing into a very tall and handsome man (who looked great on a horse and was a strong rider). He also learned to dance and dress well.

For a guy who never got a fancy education, he was doing pretty well. His ambition and hard work were paying off . . .

But in 1752 George's half brother Lawrence died of tuberculosis. George was heartbroken. It was as though Washington men were destined to die young . . .

I'm sad and probably NEXT!

Lawrence's death meant George would inherit some new land. His brother also left his former military position vacant. George decided to try and fill it.

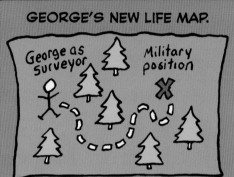

GEORGE'S NEW LIFE MAP.

George as surveyor
Military position

In 1753 George was given the title of Major Washington. His first big mission had to do with a dispute over an area of land that both the French and the British believed was theirs. George was to trek deep into the disputed territory to deliver a message to the French, "Get off our land or else!!!" (That's a paraphrase.)

After he delivered the message . . .

HA HA HA Or else what?

George had an exciting trip back home. He almost died several times.

One example involved an icy river and a raft.

Shortly after George's safe return, the dispute evolved into fighting and the "French and Indian War" was under way. George would be involved from the very start. He experienced his first loss at Fort Necessity . . .

When the British troops arrived in the colonies, they took charge of the military operations. George was placed under a General Braddock. George tried to warn the general that the fighting in America was very different from the way they fought in Europe. For instance, Europeans felt that fighting from behind trees and rocks was bad form, but in America it wasn't. General Braddock ignored George's warning, and so when they were attacked in July 1755, it was very, very ugly.

During the battle General Braddock had four horses shot from beneath him before he too was eventually shot . . .

George bravely rode about the battle like a big giant target trying to rally the troops, who were all in a panic!

By the end of the battle George had four bullet holes in his jacket and two horses had been shot from under him . . .

After the Braddock disaster George was awarded the position of Commander of the Virginia Regiment for his bravery. He was 23 years old.

In 1758 George was elected to the Virginia House of Burgess (Virginia's local government), so he resigned from his military job to move on to a new career.

GOODBYE SNIFF

GOODBYE SNIFF

HORSE ANGELS EVERYWHERE REJOICED

By the age of 26 George had shown true bravery in the face of the horrors of war. He had developed into a great leader by learning from both his mistakes and others'. All useful skills for his new career in politics, not to mention his new adventure into marriage . . .

SMOOCH

GROSS

On Jan. 6, 1759, George married Martha Custis.

WHO WAS MARTHA?

Martha was a very rich widow . . .

Jacky

Patsy

with two children from her previous marriage.

The newly married George was excited to begin his new life as a politician, a planter, and a gentleman . . .

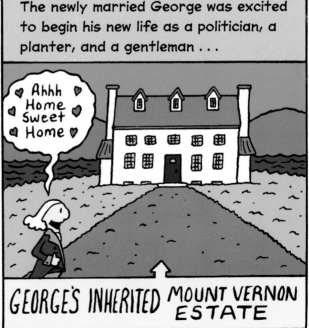

♥ Ahhh ♥ Home ♥ Sweet ♥ Home ♥

GEORGE'S INHERITED MOUNT VERNON ESTATE

For the next 16 years George and Martha lived a happy and social life. Like so many of his political peers, though, he was very aware of the behavior of the British toward the colonies.

Side note: At this point in George's life he had mastered the art of remaining cool and collected even when he was filled with passion. In 1775, when the 2nd Continental Congress decided to assume control of all the state militias to form a Continental Army, Washington was the obvious choice for its commander in chief. He accepted. Now he would have to leave his beloved family and home to stand up to British tyranny!

THE ODDS WERE GREATLY AGAINST GEORGE AND HIS ARMY.

When George arrived at Boston, he found the British troops well protected and relaxing in the city with their heavily armed boats chilling next to them in the harbor...

Before Washington had a chance to make up his mind, one of his men, Henry Knox, showed up to Boston with 58 mortars and cannons that had been captured 300 miles away at Fort Ticonderoga. It took 42 oxen-pulled sleds to get the guns to Washington!

If only he'd had a dinosaur!

Washington now had a bunch of cannons and an idea! Under cover of darkness, the army secretly moved all of the weapons to a high point called Dorchester Heights . . .

45

In the morning the British were shocked!

LOOK! CANNONS!

No way. Impossible.

THEY MUST BE FAKE.

CRASH

AGGG fake cannons

Thanks to the sneaky (but real) cannons, the British quickly hopped in their boats and left Boston to wait for reinforcements elsewhere.

Washington's next assignment was to take the army and keep New York City from being captured . . .

New York City

HUDSON RIVER

LONG ISLAND

N.Y.C. was an important access point for the Hudson River. If the British were to gain control of the Hudson, the colonists would be divided.

In the summer of 1776, the British Navy began to show up outside the city. The Americans were in trouble. They were now surrounded by water filled with the biggest, baddest navy around.

The fighting began soon after on Long Island...

BAM

BA

The fighting was intense and the Continental Army had let themselves get trapped up against the East River by the British. Things were looking bad. George had to do something quick . . .

His solution . . . another sneaky nighttime move! With the help of flat-bottomed boats and many trips, the men snuck across the river without being discovered.

Washington had escaped to fight another day, but he would lose New York City in the process . . .

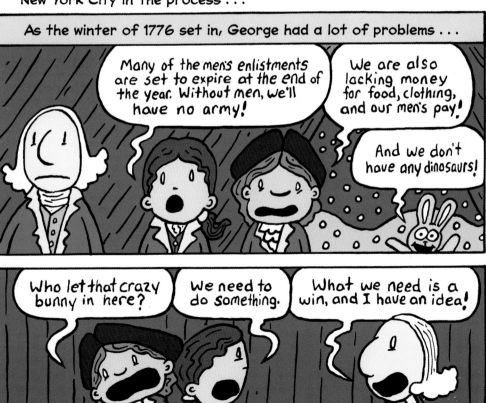

Washington's idea was to launch a surprise attack (before his men's enlistment expired) on a group of Hessians camped out in a town called Trenton. Part of the plan included a secret crossing of the Delaware River at nighttime. On the night of December 25, Washington put his risky plan into action.

Side note: Many boats were used in the crossing and several trips were made, but the idea of them using one trip in one boat is more fun to draw.

After they had crossed the Delaware River the men faced a nine-mile (quiet) hike to Trenton. Many of the soldiers lacked warm clothing and shoes. Two of the men died from the cold...

The cover of darkness was important to the plan, but they were running late and the sun was rising. They decided to attack the Hessians anyway...

EEEP

The battle was a huge success! Washington captured 900 nasty Hessians.

LOOK, NO HORNS!

The win was followed by another at Princeton, and a new energy filled the men, the Congress, and George! Even though it was a small win, it was a huge deal for an army up against such overwhelming odds . . .

The tiny wins would have to last for a while, because what followed for Washington and his men was a string of lost battles that also resulted in the loss of the current capital, Philadelphia. As the winter continued into 1777, George decided to have the army set up camp at a place called Valley Forge (it was close to Philadelphia . . . but not too close . . .).

THE WINTER WAS A COLD ONE AND THE MEN LACKED FOOD+CLOTHING...

As bad as the lack of food and clothes was, the death toll from sickness and disease was worse. Thousands would die. Valley Forge was a horrible place to be that winter. Washington did his best to encourage his troops and keep them together through the winter.

When the spring finally came, George and his army were ready to fight! Making it through a winter like that made anything seem possible, even a long drawn-out war with the British. In 1781 (4 years later) the British surrendered after the Battle of Yorktown and in 1783 the official peace treaty was signed. George had led his army to victory!

George was instantly a celebrated HERO! Everybody loved George, but because of his fame, some people were afraid that the people would want to make him king, and kings lead to tyranny.

Side note: When in public George worked hard to keep his emotions under control, but the same rules did not apply when he was with his family.

Now that the new nation had won its independence, a group of leaders wanted George to come and preside as President at the Constitutional Convention in Philadelphia. George cared deeply for his country and wanted to help, but he also was happy to be out of public life. Eventually, after a lot of thought, he decided to do it.

In 1787 the convention produced a new Constitution. It was then ratified by the 13 states (some WAY sooner than others).

Now the question was, "Who will be the first President?" That answer was the one thing everybody could agree on . . .

GEORGE!

On February 4, 1789, George Washington was elected President by the Electoral College. Congress made it official in April!

HOLD EVERYTHING! What is this Electoral College you speak of?

That's the next chapter . . .

Oh, OKAY!

When George got the message that he was to be President, he had to (once again) leave his happy place (Mount Vernon) to travel to New York City (the temporary capital). It was a huge sacrifice for George, but he did it because he loved his country. His journey to New York would make it clear his country loved him too . . .

Goodbye HOME!

SOB SOB SOB

Goodbye my George!

Side note: Buildings do not actually feel pain or cry real tears, but if they did, the above panel would be very real . . .

In every village, town, or city George passed through, he was greeted by huge crowds of cheering Americans!!!

One funny example was in Philadelphia, when George had a laurel crown placed on his head by a boy dangling from some sort of contraption.

He was then met by a crowd of 20,000 excited people.

Side note: George was a very humble man who didn't like such pageantry, but he did his best to bear it. When he could he would slip past such events, though.

On April 30, 1789, George took the presidential oath to uphold the Constitution at the Federal Hall, New York City . . .

SMOOOCH

Taking an oath with one hand on a Bible was normal, but George added a big kiss. The kiss was repeated by many Presidents after him.

Since Washington was the first President, he was responsible for many traditions that are still practiced today. In other words, he set a precedent for future Presidents.

For example, when trying to decide the official title for the office, many suggestions were made, but George made the final decision . . .

How about, "His Highness the President of the United States of America Protector of their Liberties"?

What about, "The Fabulous, Magnificent and Always Resplendently Awesome Dude"!?

NO, let's keep it simple, "President of the United States" will do...

Washington never wanted the role of President to be confused with the role a king has. So, with every decision he made, he kept that in mind.

During George's time as President he faced many challenges . . .

Such as the problem of American ships being captured by pirates!
The U.S. no longer enjoyed the protection of the British Navy.

The United States now needed its own armed ships for protection,
so in 1794 George signed the Naval Act that allowed for six ships
to be built.

When Great Britain and France
began to fight again (yes again),

some people wanted to side with
France . . . others Great Britain . . .

The French! The British! We need to help the Dinosaurs!

but Washington pushed to remain
neutral because he was afraid the
country was too young to risk
another war . . .

There is plenty more to learn about, and if you want to know more, go ask
your friendly librarian to help you find some books!

Many Americans expected that George Washington would run for President every four years until he died, but George had a different idea. After two terms (1789-1797) George was ready to call it a day and return to his wife and home . . .

Sadly, he would not get to enjoy his Mount Vernon home for long because on December 14, 1799, George died. He got ill after riding out in the rain. He did not get better.

The nation mourned its loss!

SOB SOB SOB

Over the years monument after monument has been built to honor his beloved memory ...

Some examples

Mount Rushmore

Lots of statues

The Washington Monument

and his image has popped up on everything from money to stamps to shirtless biker dudes. And in my opinion, that's a good thing.

GEORGE

NICE TATTOO

GEORGE

GEORGE

THERE IS SOOO MUCH MORE TO BE SAID ABOUT WASHINGTON...

such as,

His hair was powdered to appear white (it was not a wig).

Washington was six foot two inches tall (that was really tall for his time).

George had horrible teeth problems. He tried many different kinds of dentures over the years, but none of them were wooden.

He also had a great throwing arm! There are many tales about just how far he could throw.

Washington did value the virtue of honesty, but the story about a young George chopping down a cherry tree is likely a myth...

I cannot tell a lie

I DID IT!

UGG

OW

Many stories were exaggerations.

But we have run out of space, so it's time to move on to the next chapter! (It's about the election process.)

Chapter 3

How Does a President Get Elected?

This chapter walks us through the different elements of the presidential election process and more!!!

As we have already learned, the Constitution of the United States lays out the framework for how our three branches of government should work . . .

THE CONSTITUTION

We the People

IT'S ALL HERE ON MY BELLY!

But that's not all it does. It also details how the presidential election process should work!

So, if you have questions, I have answers !!!

Does a President get a license to kill?

I have a question, can robots be President?

I'm only seven, can I be President?

BARK BARK BARK?

MEOW?

Calm down everyone, let's give Mr. Constitution a chance to explain some basics first!

Thanks, George!

We the People

But I don't wanna listen...

George, can you throw him out of here?

We the Peo...

No problem.

UGGGG

OW

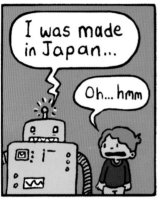

Now, the next thing written out, here on my belly, is the specifics for how the President is to be elected...

We the People

Excuse me, Mr. Constitution. Mr. Smartypants here and I don't think you need to explain how an election works. It's a simple thing—everyone casts a vote and the candidate with the most votes wins...

Sorry sir, but what you just described is a popular election, and that is not what is written on his belly.

Smart Monkey is correct!

Huh?

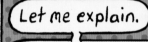

Let me explain.

You see, when the framers were making me they talked about having a popular vote, but there were some worries with that route...

The states with the biggest population will push around the smaller STATES!!!

They will elect leaders and make laws that benefit them and ignore us!

To prevent these fears from coming true...

HA HA HA

ACK

The founders created the system we call "The Electoral College."

YAY I've been waiting for a chapter for this to be explained.

I've been waiting for two chapters...

ACCCKK A TALKING BUNNY & BIRD!

Ummm... didn't he notice he was talking to ink on paper before...

Right again, Monkey.

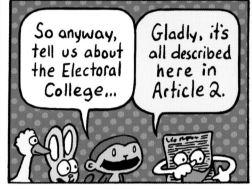

So anyway, tell us about the Electoral College...

Gladly, it's all described here in Article 2.

Right here?

HA HA HA STOP! that tickles...

Thanks. Now, Article 2 begins by asking the states to do a math problem...

The states have to add together the number of senators they have with the number of representatives they have... The total equals the number of electors the state gets...

Senate (always 2) ➕ Representatives (based on state's population) 🟰 # of electors ✳

✳ From here on out, electors will be represented by HAMSTERS.

64

Every four years each state holds their very own presidential election, where everyone who can vote is free to do so . . .

Once all the votes are in, the states then assign their electors to go and cast their votes for whoever won the state's popular vote.

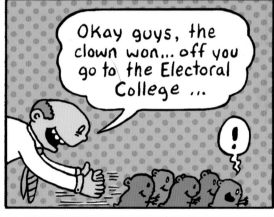

Side note: A few states have a slightly different process than the one described here... Is your state one of them?

The candidate who gets more than 50% of the electoral vote is declared THE WINNER!

Here's a current Electoral College map of the United States.

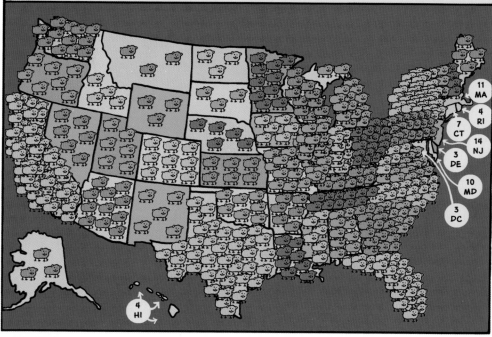

Any questions?

What happens if there is an electoral tie?

If there is a tie, the House of Representatives will break it. Each State's representatives get 1 vote to cast as a group, but it has only happened once, in the year 1800!*

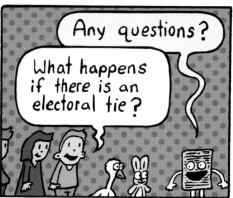

Could somebody win the popular vote nation wide but still lose the election?

Yup, that happened in 1824, 1876, 1888, and in 2000... but remember, there is a reason for the system.

BIG POPULOUS STATE CRUSH!

EECK

* This is also the process used if no candidate gets more than 50% of the vote.

When the framers created this system, how did they know it would work?

They didn't, but that's what the amendment process is for!

For example, the tied 1800 election brought to light a few problems that were eventually fixed by the Twelfth Amendment...

NICE

We the People

So, do you guys feel like you have a basic understanding of the Electoral College now?

Yes, I can now die a happy duck

When's the next election? I want to vote!

Sorry, bunnies and ducks can't vote.

ARGGGGGG

But that does bring up a good question...

WHO GETS TO VOTE IN PRESIDENTIAL ELECTIONS?

SOB SOB SOB

There, there, bunny

We the People

67

The truth is I didn't, originally, say much about who could or couldn't vote. Those decisions were left mostly to the states...

In America's early years most states required a voter to be a landowner...

SINCE I OWN LAND I CAN VOTE!

I TOO OWN LAND. SO I CAN VOTE!

NO YOU DON'T, YOU'RE JUST HOLDING A PIECE OF DIRT FROM MY LAND!

But by the mid-1800s this requirement had faded away.

YAY

As you probably know, many states once had rules that didn't allow non-whites or women to vote... Thankfully, many people fought long and hard to bring about change...

and slowly I have been amended to guarantee that people cannot be disqualified to vote based on their race, sex, or color!

Here's a quick look at a few of the improvements made to our voting rules...

THE **14th** Amendment 1868

One of the things this amendment did was to produce an official definition of what a United States citizen was. It made it very clear that newly free slaves were indeed citizens...(Before the Civil War, the Supreme Court claimed slaves were not United States citizens.)

THE **15th** Amendment 1870

The 15th Amendment made it illegal to prevent somebody from voting based only on their race or color!!!

In the years following the Civil War (1861-1865) many states and local governments still wanted to keep former slaves from voting. So they enforced tough requirements to vote. They used things like poll taxes to try and prevent free but still mostly poor black Americans from voting.

I'm here to vote.

Poll tax, Please.

How much?

One dollar more than you have.

It would take almost 100 years of protests and legal fights to fix these problems.

THE **19th** Amendment 1920

This amendment allowed women the right to vote!!!

YAY YAY YAY

THE
23rd
Amendment
1961

Since the United States capital is not officially in a state, the people who live in it weren't able to take part in the presidential elections... but this amendment fixed it so that now they can.

YAY! YAY! YAY!

Still doesn't help me...

THE
24th
Amendment
1964

This amendment prevents poll taxes and any other taxes required for people to vote.

THE
26th
Amendment
1971

Because an 18-year-old can serve in the military, it made sense to lower the voting age to 18. (In some states it was 21.)

NOW I CAN VOTE FOR MY COMMANDER IN CHIEF!

There is so much more that could be said on this topic but, alas, it's time to move on...

But just in case you are sad because turning 18 seems so far away, at least you can be happy that you're not a bunny!

HA HA HA HA HA

SNIFF

Now that we know who can run for President and who can vote, it's time to look at what presidential hopefuls need to do to get elected.

In its essence it's actually pretty simple . . . A presidential candidate needs to communicate to the voters why he or she would be a great President.

Sometimes it helps for a candidate to have a catchy slogan that sums stuff up. Below are some past presidents' slogans and a bunny fail.

VOTE YOURSELF A FARM.	A CHICKEN IN EVERY POT AND A CAR IN EVERY GARAGE.	ARE YOU BETTER OFF THAN YOU WERE FOUR YEARS AGO?	A CAR IN EVERY POT AND A CHICKEN IN EVERY GARAGE.
Abraham Lincoln Election of 1860	Herbert Hoover Election of 1928	Ronald Reagan Election of 1980	Bunny can't run

Of course, it gets a little more complicated because there can only be one President and it's a big country, so, what naturally happens is . . .

people who share the same ideas and visions team up and work together.

WE CALL THESE GROUPS POLITICAL PARTIES...

Usually, during elections you will see that there are two dominant political parties. These parties are filled with members who hold a wide range of views, but they have enough in common that they can work together to try and win that hard-to-get 51% of the electoral vote.

TODAY THE TWO BIGGEST PARTIES ARE...

The Republican Party **AND** The Democratic Party

MASCOT - The Elephant

MASCOT - The Donkey

But that hasn't always been the case . . .

Throughout the U.S.A.'s history there have been many different parties (here are just a few).		
THE FEDERALIST PARTY	THE DEMOCRATIC-REPUBLICAN PARTY	
THE WHIG PARTY	THE SOCIAL DEMOCRAT PARTY	
THE CONSTITUTION PARTY		
THE AMERICAN FIRST PARTY	THE GREEN PARTY	
	THE LIBERTARIAN PARTY	

Before a presidential election takes place each party gets together and decides who will represent them as their presidential candidate.

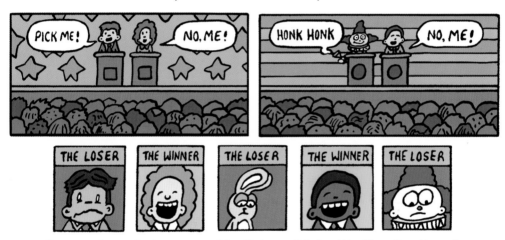

Once each party has a presidential candidate, it's time for them to

Fight it out !!!

No, they fight each other with their words and ideas because they are trying to win votes, not get arrested for assault with a deadly chicken.

Getting your message out to the American people is a huge task, even with the help of a big political party and lots of money—and it takes a lot of money.

"So, how do they do it?" you ask. Well, there are plenty of ways . . .

One way is to hit the campaign trail and visit the states in person, giving speeches about "who you are" and "what you stand for" . . . (in addition to the bonus of letting people see that you are not a robot).

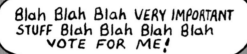

> Blah Blah Blah VERY IMPORTANT STUFF Blah Blah Blah Blah VOTE FOR ME!

> What did you think?

> I've changed my mind. He's not a robot.

Shaking hands and kissing babies helps too.

Candidates can also do interviews in any number of different kinds of media . . .

PRINT | ONLINE | RADIO | T.V.

CMM news

> SO, JOE, THE BIG QUESTION ON EVERYONE'S MIND IS, ARE YOU A ROBOT?

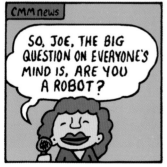

CMM news

> HMMM... BEEP BOP BOOP... COMPUTING... ANSWER... BEEP YES

CMM news

> JUST KIDDING, I AM NOT A ROBOT

> HA HA HA

Humor helps too . . . If it's actually funny . . .

Sometimes the leading candidates will meet and debate each other about tough issues. This gives people a great chance to see both candidates in action under pressure . . .

AND THOSE WERE MY 157 REASONS FOR SUPPORTING THAT LAW!

I DISAGREE WITH JENNY FOR 184 REASONS, NUMBER 1...

The debates usually have time limits to keep politicians from going on and on and on . . .

Z Z Z Z Z Z

During election season you will notice signs going up everywhere.

Their purpose is to make sure you never forget a candidate's name EVEN IN YOUR SLEEP!

The commercials will invade the media . . .

I'm for the little guy!

Where'd my cartoons go?

JOE FOR PRESIDENT

Sometimes the ads will even go negative. For better or worse, there is a long tradition of mean ads throughout presidential history.

FACT ⊂ When Jenny was little she believed in unicorns! ⊂ Only CRAZY people believe in unicorns !!!

Joe says he's for the little guy...

but he's 6 foot 4! How can he be for the little guy?

6
5
4

* These ads were brought to you by friends of Bunny.

The campaign possibilities are truly endless . . .

but because money isn't endless, the parties usually stick with what they believe works best.

In the end, it all comes down to the voters and what they want and who they think can deliver!!!

It really can be a crazy process, but at least we have free elections. Many countries have only one political party in power, so be thankful.

Eventually the presidential election day will arrive and the people's voices will be heard. Those who are registered and qualified to vote will go their polling place and cast their secret ballot.

Early in America's history, the vote wasn't always a secret. It was often verbal. This practice was ended to prevent intimidation!

Once all the votes are counted and one candidate gets over 50% of the electoral vote, the winner is declared!!!

On Jan 20, the new President officially begins his job.

I DO SOLEMNLY SWEAR THAT I WILL FAITHFULLY EXECUTE THE OFFICE OF PRESIDENT OF THE UNITED STATES, AND WILL TO THE BEST OF MY ABILITY PRESERVE, PROTECT, AND DEFEND THE CONSTITUTION OF THE UNITED STATES.

It's a huge deal to take on the task of protecting the Constitution, but luckily the President isn't alone in this, because the Supreme Court and the Congress also make pledges to protect it.

Over the next 4 years the new President will be carefully watched by voters and the media to see if he upholds his campaign promises and how he performs his job.

Arggg. It's been 2 years and there is still no car in my pot...

UM

You made that promise, not the current President.

GRRR

You're right... I need to go for a drive... have you seen where I put the keys to my chicken?

SIGH

And for those who aren't happy with the way things turned out on Election Day, there is wonderful news: The game is not over, it never is... there are constantly new government officials up for elections in Congress in your state, and in four years there will be another presidential election!!!

As we bring this section to a close, some of you may be crying and thinking aloud...

Look at it this way: You have lots of time to become a thoughtful and well-informed voter!

You can learn more about the Constitution,

read more about American history,

and learn all about different political parties and current events.

So, when the day comes that you can vote, you will be totally prepared and ready to take part in your American privilege.

Chapter 4

Why Is the White House So Awesome?

This chapter is an introduction to the building that serves as a home and a place of work for the President!

In this chapter our goal is to...

GET TO KNOW THE WHITE HOUSE.

Because the White House is over 200 years old, there are plenty of things we could learn about it, but it would probably be most helpful to start off with some basics . . .

The White House is located at 1600 Pennsylvania Avenue in Washington, D.C. It's the place where the P.O.T.U.S. both lives and works (yes, at the same time).

Luckily, the framers knew that they would need a capital city with buildings to house the new federal government (including the President). So they gave the government the authority to build one in the Constitution (Article 1, Section 8), but first they would need to agree on where to build it...

Eventually, after some compromises, a location was settled on . . .

The location was a spot between Virginia and Maryland.

It was named Washington.

81

The next step was to plan out the city. French architect/artist Charles L'Enfant was chosen for the job.

I plan cities!

Sadly, due to disagreements with his design, Charles was fired and there were still no designs for the President's house. Thomas Jefferson came to the rescue with a solution...

I have an idea!

I propose...

We have a competition between several architects...

and George Washington will pick the winner.

THE WINNER

PANT PANT PANT

FINISH

You look confused... Let me rephrase.

I propose we have a contest where architects will present their designs and George will pick the winner.

Oh, I get it now...

Jefferson's idea was adopted.

George likes!

The winning design was by architect James Hoban. The winning design: a Georgian mansion in the Palladian style.

Palladian is my favorite

Me too...

Construction of the President's home and office began in 1792.

WOW! THIS VIRGINIA SANDSTONE IS SOOO GRAY!

I BET THEY CALL THIS PLACE THE GRAY HOUSE!

In 1798 the sandstone walls were whitewashed.

NOW WHAT WILL THEY CALL IT?

I HAVE NO CLUE.

In 1800 the first official resident President moved into the nearly finished structure...

AHHH... HOME SWEET HOME!

2nd President of the U.S.
John Adams
1797-1801

Unfortunately for President Adams his stay would be very short because he had just lost his bid for re-election to his rival.

AHHH... HOME SWEET HOME!

SIGH

3rd President of the U.S.
Thomas Jefferson
1801-1809

George Washington would be the only President who would not make the White House his temporary home, but at least he played a large role in its being built before he died.

Of course, it's worth mentioning that the White House was not officially called the White House yet ... It actually had many different names.

Hey Look, THE PRESIDENT'S HOUSE!

The what?

Oh, you mean the Executive Mansion.

No, I think he means the Presidential Palace!

No, it's called the White House...

formerly Known as the Gray House.

It would take about 100 years for the White House to be officially called the White House. How did it become official, you ask?

Well, in 1901, President Theodore Roosevelt (1901-1909) put that name on the top of his official stationery!

THE WHITE HOUSE

Clearly, stationery has great powers!

BEFORE STATIONERY

Hi, Jim

AFTER STATIONERY

Hi, Super-Awesome Intelligent and Handsome Dude!

Now that we've learned some White House basics, let's take a look at HOW THE WHITE HOUSE HAS GROWN AND CHANGED OVER THE YEARS

You see, just like humans grow and change . . .

So too do buildings . . . just not in the same way.

Buildings grow and change in different ways.

Examples:

Technological advances

Additions

Remodels

Since the White House is really, really old, it has undergone a lot of changes. The next few pages will take a look at a few of them . . .

One of the first changes was partly due to laundry problems . . .

Abigail Adams (the 2nd President's wife) didn't think it was proper to be a public official and have your laundry hanging where just anyone could see it.

LOOK! THE PRESIDENT'S COW!

LOOK! THE PRESIDENT'S UNDERWEAR!

Because her stay in the White House would be short, Abigail chose a short-term solution. She hung her clothes up inside the unfinished East Room . . .

It would be the next President's job to solve this privacy problem.

And solve it President Jefferson did. How? By designing (with the help of Benjamin Henry Latrobe) and adding a colonnade to each side of the White House. Privacy was improved a little . . .

In 1812 the U.S.A. and Great Britain were at war again (it was called the War of 1812). One of the casualties of the war would be the White House and a large part of the capital city . . . In 1814 the British captured Washington and set a major portion of it ablaze.

(Sources say that Dolley had plenty of help, but it's more fun to draw it this way.)
This event spurred a lot of change for the White House, both good and bad.
The Bad = being destroyed
The Good = being rebuilt all brand-new (1815-1817)

James Hoban (the original architect) was invited back to assist with the rebuilding . . . (he was not dead yet).

The next two big changes for the White House were two new porticos.

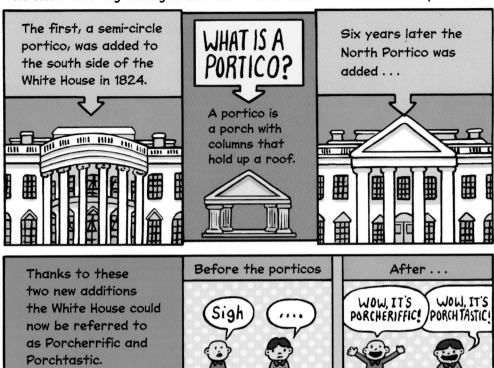

The first, a semi-circle portico, was added to the south side of the White House in 1824.

WHAT IS A PORTICO?

A portico is a porch with columns that hold up a roof.

Six years later the North Portico was added . . .

Thanks to these two new additions the White House could now be referred to as Porcherrific and Porchtastic.

Before the porticos

Sigh

. . . .

After . . .

WOW, IT'S PORCHERIFFIC!

WOW, IT'S PORCHTASTIC!

In addition to the building's many improvements thus far, the 1800s also brought a lot of technological advances (many of them were way ahead of their time for normal American homes).

A few examples . . .

The 1830s brought running water.

The 1840s brought gas lights.

And the late 1870s brought the first telephone.

RING

FUN FACT

The White House's first phone # was 1.

YAY!

That's right just 1 . . .

IN YOUR FACE, 8!

TAKE THAT, 7!

Seriously, just the # 1.

HEY, 9, GUESS WHAT!

87

In 1891 the White House got electric lights!	But not everyone was a big fan right away ...
Somebody, turn on the lights! NOOO! DON'T!	Don't touch that switch or you might become a Burnt Krispy!

The President at the time was Benjamin Harrison, and both he and his wife were deathly afraid that the light switches would electrocute anyone who touched them.

In 1902 President Theodore Roosevelt needed some more office space, so he had some built on the west side of the White House. It was called the West Wing. Over the years it has been remodeled and changed several times.

THE WEST WING

Home of the Oval Office.

In 1942 an East Wing was added to the White House. This addition added more offices and hid construction of a secret bunker being built underneath.

THE EAST WING

Home of the not so secret bunker.

Now the White House had a lot in common with ...

ostriches and penguins...

Huh?

They all have two wings and can't fly.

HA HA HA HA

In 1949 it was discovered that the White House really needed some new internal reinforcements when . . .

President Truman's daughter's piano partly fell through the floor.

I'm SOOOO done practicing.

So, from 1949-1952 President Truman and his family moved across the street while most of the White House was gutted and rebuilt with a steel structure. Two basements were added as well.

That's a DROP!

Thanks to the new basements, there would be room for President Nixon (1969-1974) to add a bowling alley!!!

It wasn't actually the first bowling alley. There was also one built in 1947, but it was short-lived due to lack of space. There is plenty more that could be said about the White House building, but for now let's end this topic with the bowling alley and move on to different aspects of life in the White House.

LIFE IN THE WHITE HOUSE!

THE WHITE HOUSE AS A PLACE OF WORK!

In today's modern White House, most of the business side of things are done in the West Wing.

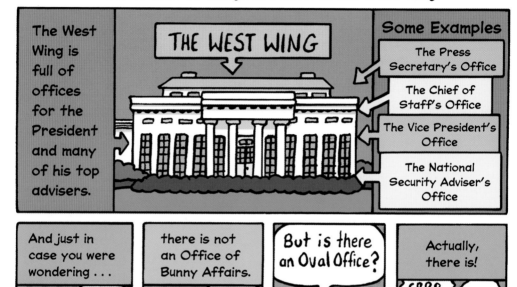

The West Wing is full of offices for the President and many of his top advisers.

THE WEST WING

Some Examples

The Press Secretary's Office

The Chief of Staff's Office

The Vice President's Office

The National Security Adviser's Office

And just in case you were wondering . . .

I am.

there is not an Office of Bunny Affairs.

Oh... Sniff

But is there an Oval Office?

Actually, there is!

GRRR   YAY!

The Oval Office is actually the President's office. It is called the Oval Office because it is shaped like an oval . . .

Oh... SNIFF

HA HA HA

The Oval Office

MY OFFICE!

Not my office.

In addition to the many individual offices, the West Wing is also home to a few other rooms.

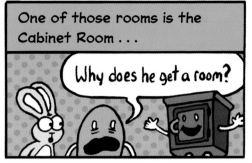

One of those rooms is the Cabinet Room . . .

Why does he get a room?

He doesn't. It's not that type of Cabinet Room . . .

Oh... SNIFF

It is a conference room for the President and his advisers to talk turkey.

GOBBLE GOBBLE GOBBLE

CABINET ROOM

There is another room for talking called the Situation Room.

This room is more than just any old conference room, because it is hooked up to talk to important leaders all over the world at once . . .

IS ANYONE ELSE HAVING BUNNY PROBLEMS?

The West Wing is also home to a room for the reporters to hang out in and another for press conferences...

MR. PRESIDENT, WHY DON'T YOU RESPECT BUNNIES?

OR OVALS?

The White House can be a very stressful place at times, and a hardworking President will often need to take a moment to stop, relax, and, perhaps, smell the roses . . . or they could just do what President Coolidge (1923-1929) liked to do when he needed some relief . . . push a bunch of secret buttons . . .

Of course, there are plenty of ways to relax at the White House, and that can include spending time with one's family.

LIFE IN THE WHITE HOUSE!

THE WHITE HOUSE AS A HOME!

Sometimes it's easy to forget that from its very beginning, the White House has been a home for the President and his or her family. And whenever a home contains a family, it will surely be filled with drama, love, funny stories, and so much more. The White House is no different.

President Theodore Roosevelt (1901-1909) had a large family in the White House.

FAMILY

One day when one of the little ones was sick and stuck in bed...

COUGH COUGH

DRAMA

His brothers and sisters decided to try and cheer him up by sneaking his favorite horse to his upstairs room... it worked.

LOVE

YAY! COUGH

FUNNY

Another good story involves President Andrew Johnson (1865-1869) and his daughter Martha's war on rats.

FAMILY

You see, the White House had a rat problem...

DRAMA

Martha did her best to fix the problem...

DIE RATS

FUNNY

But her father liked the critters...

Dinner time my fluffy muffins!

LOVE

Being over 200 years old, the White House has filled entire books with wonderful family stories, but this is not one of those books . . . for we must move on to learn other important stuff, like where exactly the First Family lives in the really old house . . .

In the modern White House the First Family's main home is in part of the 2nd floor.

The rest of the building is full of museum-like rooms (many of which have color themes).

some examples

The Green Room (The Booger Room)

The Blue Room (The Alien Booger Room)

The Red Room (The Bloody Nose Room)

Adult names above, unofficial childish names below . . .

These rooms have their purposes, but they prove very boring to Presidents' kids . . .

Found it! Now, it's your turn!

No thanks...I'm tired of playing Hide the Lemon.

Luckily for the First Kids, the White House is also home to an indoor movie theater, an outdoor pool, a bowling alley, and so much more . . .

The Yellow Oval Room (The Zit Cream Room)

The White House children are not allowed to complain.

Yum

oooo

Now that we know where the family lives and that the kids can have fun, the only important question left is . . . "Are pets allowed in the White House?" The simple answer is, "Of course!" In fact, almost every President has had at least one pet. But some Presidents have had personal ZOOs. If you want to know

which President has had the most pets, it's probably a toss-up between . . .

| President Theodore Roosevelt 1901-1909 | AND | President Calvin Coolidge 1923-1929 |

But if one had to choose a winner, President Coolidge would get the award because he had a pygmy hippo named Billy, and pygmy hippos are awesome!!!

LIFE IN THE WHITE HOUSE!

THE WHITE HOUSE AS A FANCY PANTS PLACE!

In case you were wondering how those museum-like rooms serve a purpose, the President uses them as nice places to meet with . . .

Important leaders . . . and . . . people with fancy pants.

BLAH BLAH BLAH

BLAH BLAH BLAH BLAH

BLAH

The White House also has a fancy large room called the East Room. It is used for dances, banquets, concerts, roller-skating, hanging laundry, and much, much more . . .

There is also a fancy "State Dining Room" in the White House (another fancy place for eating).

TONIGHT'S MAIN COURSE WILL BE ROASTED PYGMY HIPPO!

JUST KIDDING, BILLY. IT'S RABBIT.

SIGH

HAHAHA

In modern times one needs an invitation to go to a fancy event at the White House, but it hasn't always been this way. President Andrew Jackson (1829-1837) wanted to open his inauguration celebration (his "I won the election party") to anyone who wanted to show up . . . The party quickly got out of hand.

The people had to be lured outside with drinks and snacks.

LOOK! Refreshments!

When all was said and done, the White House had been trashed. Sadly, those partiers ruined it for the rest of us, but if you ever do get a chance to hang out in the White House, make your way to the Lincoln Bedroom, where, rumor has it, if you make a wish while lying on the Lincoln bed, your wish will come true.

The Lincoln Bedroom

I wish this chapter was over...

WAIT NO That was a dumb wish... can I wish for a Million dollars instead?

NOPE, too LATE.

END OF WHITE HOUSE CHAPTER

Chapter 5

What Do Presidents Actually Do?

This chapter will take a look at different duties of a President (and more).

The purpose of this chapter is to take a much closer look at what the President's job actually requires . . . But first, let's review some of the things we have already learned about the job . . .

For starters... To get elected President, one must first campaign long and hard, telling the American people what you believe and what you stand for...

I am Frank and I hate annoying bunnies and tyranny, but I love America and Americans! And as Americans...

FRANK FOR PRESIDENT

FRANK FOR PRESIDENT

LET ME BE FRANK

we must never forget to value our freedoms and forever be ready to protect them from Tyranny!

PLUS, I AM NOT A ROBOT!

YAY!

ONE MUST ALSO KISS A LOT OF BABIES...

SMOOCH

You have a beautiful baby. VOTE FOR ME!

WAAAAAA

Sigh

The elected President must take the Oath of Office (to uphold and protect the Constitution).

Then the President (along with family and pets) can move into the White House.

Protect me!

GET YE BACK, TYRANNY!

Come on, Shampoo, we're almost to the pool.

WHALES MAKE BAD PETS.

NOW HE OR SHE IS READY TO BEGIN THE JOB...

WAIT A SECOND... The job doesn't begin till I have my morning cup of coffee.

Siiiiip

Siiiiiiiiiip

Siiiiiiiiiiiiiiip

AHHH!

OKAY ALL DONE.

LET'S GET THIS ON LIKE WASHINGTON

NOW ... he or she is ready to begin the job ...

And now that the review is over, we are ready to take a closer look at the job of President and its MANY DUTIES . . .

THE PRESIDENT AS FOREIGN POLICY GUY...

One of the President's jobs is to build happy and fantastic relationships with other countries.

One way the President can do this is by picking good people to go to other countries to represent the United States government. These people are called ambassadors.

HEY BOB, WANNA BE AN AMBASSADOR?

I DO!

The Constitution gives the President the authority to pick a candidate for ambassador, but the Senate must approve of the choice.

WE APPROVE

WHEEEEE

GREETINGS WAMBOLLIA! TAKE ME TO YOUR LEADER.

The President is also expected to meet with ambassadors and leaders that other countries send to the U.S.A. (This isn't always easy, because different countries have different customs.)

OKAY, the proper way to greet the MOAGWI AMBASSADOR is to slap him in the face with this fish, then scream...

"WALA WALA PIGGY WIGGIE!"

...OKAY

SLAP

WALA WALA Piggy Wiggie

So, how'd I do?

Great... except that wasn't the ambassador!

Then who was that?

I DON'T KNOW, BUT HE SURE LOOKS ANGRY!

Sometimes when the President is meeting with the world leaders, he takes them to his own special retreat called . . .

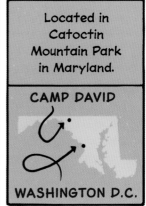

It is a place where important work can get done.
It is also a great place to relax and play . . .

Sometimes the President will visit foreign leaders in their own countries. It's easy to do when you have your very own plane.
Quick note: Any plane the President is on is called "Air Force One."

Constantly meeting with world leaders may seem like a really cool part of the job at first, but over time the endless hand-shaking and fancy dull ceremonies will start to become very tiresome. But there is an upside: People meeting with the President love to bring gifts!!!

From paintings to tea sets, Presidents get loads of gifts from around the world.

Here are just a few great examples ⤵

Our 6th President, John Quincy Adams (1825-1829), received a pet alligator from the Marquis de Lafayette!

Our 41st President, George H. W. Bush (1989-1993), received a Komodo dragon as a gift from the President of Indonesia.

Our 42nd President, Bill Clinton (1993-2001), received a rug with his and his wife's faces weaved into it, from the President of Azerbaijan.

SOCKS, DON'T STEP ON MY FACE!

Our 19th President, Rutherford B. Hayes (1877-1881), received "The Resolute Desk" from Queen Victoria in 1880 . . .

The Resolute Desk was made from the H.M.S. *Resolute* (a ship that got stuck in ice, was abandoned, but was later rescued and returned to Great Britain by the U.S.). It was a thoughtful gift!

It has been used by many Presidents as their Oval Office desk since.

It should be mentioned that because of the nature of our government, the founders were reluctant to allow Presidents to receive gifts. So, they wrote into the Constitution that gifts had to be approved by the Congress.

This provision deeply upset President Martin Van Buren (1837-1841) because Congress decided to make him give his two tiger cubs (gifts from the Sultan of Oman) to a ZOO . . .

GOOD-BYE MY BABIES!

ZOO

The last foreign policy duty of the President that we will mention here is that he or she is in charge of making treaties (written agreements) with other countries. For a treaty to be official it has to be approved by 2/3 of the Senate and the President.

A Treaty Example

After the United States had won its independence from Great Britain in 1783, it was still having problems with them.

One of the big problems was that the British were capturing U.S. ships and forcing the sailors to join the British military to fight the French.

GOTCHA

BUT WE'RE AMERICANS!

HA HA HA NO YOU'RE NOT.

President George Washington sent an American statesman named John Jay to England to try and solve the problems.

TO ENGLAND

Side note: He probably took a boat.

Jay went to England and returned with a proposed treaty that solved some of the problems. The Senate approved it and George signed it in 1795 . . .

It became known as "Jay's Treaty."

That's me!

It was not a popular treaty with the American people. They felt it left the U.S.A. on the losing side of things, but it did accomplish what George wanted it to do. It avoided a war with Great Britain . . .

Did I say that was me? I meant, my name is Bob.

GRR RRR

Now we move on to another part of the President's job . . .

THE PRESIDENT AS COMMANDER IN CHIEF

Being commander in chief means that the President is the top leader of the United States military.

Yes, being commander in chief is a very important job. And although it is generally accepted that the President has the power to repel invasions, he does not have the power to declare war. That power belongs only to Congress.

Another duty of the President, as commander in chief, is to always be ready to use the "Nuclear Football." So, "What is this 'Nuclear Football'?" you ask. Well, it's either . . .

The Answer is B: The "Nuclear Football" is the name used for a suitcase that contains codes that, when entered, would give the go-ahead for the use of nuclear weapons. You see, if the terrible need for such force ever did come up, it would do so quickly. That is why the President must be near the football at all times.

Although this book makes silly jokes about everything, the use of a nuclear bomb is a very serious thing. They cause tremendous, long-lasting, and horrifying damage. The reality of this specific presidential power should not be taken lightly.

The President also has the duty to appoint Supreme Court justices and federal judges. His appointments must be approved by a majority of the Senate before they become official. (We actually already learned this.)

The President makes a pick . . .	The Senate thinks about it . . .	If approved . . .	

In addition to that, the President is in charge of appointing people to be heads of the different executive departments. There are currently 15 departments that assist the President with his or her job, but once again, the position must be approved by a majority of the Senate.

The President makes a pick . . .	The Senate thinks about it . . .	If approved . . .	

Yes, the President is in charge of appointing lots of positions. This can make life difficult at times . . .

The Constitution also asks that the President inform Congress (from time to time) about the "State of the Union."

In addition to being able to recommend laws to Congress, the President also has "Veto Power."

WHAT IS VETO POWER?

Veto Power is a power the President gets from the Constitution.

The power is to be used as a "check" on the law-making process.

The power gives the President the ability to stop a bill from becoming a law . . . (by sending it back to Congress).

If the President vetoes a bill, Congress has 3 choices . . .

(A) They can change the bill and try again.

(B) They can just give up.

(C) Or they can overturn the President's veto, if they can get 2/3 of both Houses to vote for the Bill.

So, as you can see, the President's veto power gives him or her a lot of influence in the law-making process.

Another interesting power the Constitution gives the President is the power to pardon people who have committed federal crimes. (This means the President can let federal criminals off the hook for their crimes or reduce their sentence.)

An example of a Presidential Pardon: During George Washington's presidency, the federal government added a tax on whiskey that made a lot of farmers in the Western Pennsylvania area very upset!!!

The farmers were not very nice to those who were from the government.

The rebellion quickly grew into an armed resistance, but when President Washington responded by heading to Western PA with an army, the rebellion fell apart.

Two of the rebel leaders were arrested and convicted of treason and sentenced to death, but Washington pardoned them!

In addition to granting pardons, Presidents can also take part in the tradition to pardon the Thanksgiving turkey destined for the White House dinner.

I officially pardon you, turkey.

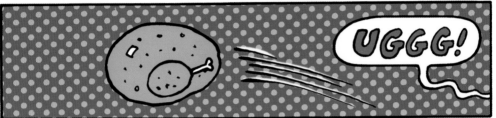
UGGG!

YOU'RE FREE NOW! FREE!!!

The whole idea is to pardon the turkey before you cook it...

Ohh... Heh...

So far, we have learned that the job of President comes with a lot of POWER and RESPONSIBILITIES, but we haven't yet learned about some of the physical dangers that come along with the job, SUCH AS . . .

The hard to avoid hand strain that comes with excessive hand-shaking and signature making . . .

The constant stresses of the job and tiny, tiny print on documents will strain your eyes and give you tragic headaches!!!

Ummm... so far these physical dangers don't seem so bad...

SADLY, IT GETS WORSE. THERE IS ALSO THE DANGER OF DEATH!

Oh my, you mean there are people out there who want to hurt the President?

YES

You see, sometimes, people who disagree with the President (which is allowed) decide to try and end the disagreement by hurting the President (which is not allowed). And sometimes people try to hurt the President because they are crazy in the head (either way, it is still wrong).

The following is a brief look at each assassination . . .

 The 2nd President to be assassinated was James A. Garfield.

1881 — 1881

Garfield was shot twice in a crowded railway station in Washington, D.C., by a man named Charles J. Guiteau.

BAM BAM EEEK

His death was all the more tragic because it was slow. He was shot on July 2, 1881, but he didn't die until September 19 . . .

His assassin turned out to be a very delusional man who believed that he had been wronged by the President.

But I was! I deserved a diplomatic appointment!

He believed the President had only been elected because of *his* hard work and a spectacular speech he had written . . .

It's true. I'm awesome. My words could get a bunny elected.

really?

Charles Guiteau was put on trial, found guilty, then hanged till dead.

 The 3rd President to be assassinated was William McKinley.

1897 — 1901

When visiting the Pan-American Exposition (a really big fair) in Buffalo, N.Y., President McKinley was also shot twice . . .

BAM BAM EEEK

The shooter was quickly tackled.

McKinley was heard to have said, "Go easy on him, boys."

McKinley would suffer for eight days before he died.

UG

The shooter, Leon Czolgosz, turned out to be a socialist-anarchist. He didn't like America's form of government.

He was put on trial, found guilty, and sentenced to death.

 The last President to be assassinated was John F. Kennedy.

1961 — 1963

He was shot by a sniper while riding in a motorcade through Dallas, Texas. Of the shots fired, two found their mark.

BAM
BAM
BAM
EEE

A man named Lee Harvey Oswald was arrested for the crime (after he shot a police officer).

Before Oswald could stand trial, he was shot by a man named Jack Ruby while being moved to a jail.

ARGGG

BAM

In addition to the four assassinations, there are also many stories of failed assassination attempts . . .

Sadly, a robo-suit is not practical (yet) and as we know, politicians don't want to appear to be robots . . . but don't you worry, even though a President can never be 100% protected, there is a group of men and women who are currently doing a great job at keeping the President safe.

They are called the Secret Service.

They arrive at places before the President to make sure it is safe.

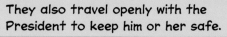

They also travel openly with the President to keep him or her safe.

Plus they protect the President from behind the scenes . . .

And they investigate presidential threats . . .

The Secret Service was originally created (in 1865) to stop counterfeiters.

Counterfeiters are people who make

 also known as funny money, or in this case bunny money.

When it became clear that the President was in need of protection, the Secret Service was given the task. Over time their role as "brave protectors" has expanded to include . . .

The President and family	The Vice President and family	Visiting heads of state	Candidates for V.P. and P.	Retired Presidents

Now that we have learned of the dangerous side of the presidency, it is time to learn about another downside to being President. Presidents get very little privacy. Their day-to-day life is now of great interest to everyone . . . especially the embarrassing stuff.

So, if you get stuck in a tub, like President Taft did . . .

Uh-oh

Or, get photographed freaking out over a swimming rabbit like President Carter did . . .

EEEK

Or throw up at a state dinner like President George H. W. Bush did . . .

THE WORLD WILL PROBABLY FIND OUT... So, future Presidents be warned.

*And now . . . Because this is the longest chapter in this book, the author wanted to give you a quick break with two pages of cute animals relaxing with milk shakes!

And now back to the chapter . . .

Another important duty of the President is to always obey the rule of law ... You see, even as President you are not "Above the Law." (Unless you are standing on a statue of the word "Law." Then you are above it ...)

President Ulysses S. Grant (1869-1877) was reminded of this when he was pulled over and ticketed for speeding. He paid the fine.

STOP
Clippitty Cloppitty Clippitty Cloppitty Clippitty Clip

Clippitty Cloppitty...Clop.. clip......Clo clip...... clip......

YOUR TICKET, MR. PRESIDENT
Sigh

If the President were to commit a much more serious wrongdoing, he or she could be fired. The Constitution lays out how this would work.

First, the President needs to be charged with misconduct (this happens in the House of Representatives).

I accuse the President of stealing the Washington Monument and selling it to evil aliens!

If a majority of the House of Representatives finds the charges against the President credible, they can vote to impeach the President. (In this instance, impeach just means that the charges against the President are now official.)

So, what do you think?
Sounds credible
Let's impeach the President

AND MAKE HIM WEAR THIS FUNNY HAT!

IMPEACHED

Who let that crazy bunny in here?

Once a President has been impeached, he or she must then stand trial. This part takes place in the Senate.

Once the trial is finished, 2/3 of the Senate must vote to convict the President to make it official. If convicted, the President is no longer the President. In the U.S.A.'s history two Presidents have been impeached (Presidents Andrew Johnson and Bill Clinton), but neither was convicted by the Senate.

SO, IF THE PRESIDENT IS NO LONGER PRESIDENT, THEN WHO IS THE PRESIDENT?

Good question, Mr. Hamster. If the President is no longer able to do the job because of . . .

Death	serious injury,	he or she quits	or is fired...
BURP	Groan	I QUIT	YOU'RE Fired

The Constitution places the Vice President next in line . . .

If something were to happen to him or her,

GRRRR

EEECK BURP

The Constitution allows for Congress to create an extended list of who's next in line. And make a list they did (it gets changed from time to time).

*Vice President
*Speaker of the House
*President pro tempore of the Senate
*Secretary of State

*Secretary of the Treasury
*Secretary of Defense
*Attorney General
*Secretary of the Interior

*Secretary of Agriculture
*Secretary of Commerce
*Secretary of Labor
*Secretary of Health and Human Services

*Secretary of Housing and Urban Development
*Secretary of Transportation
*Secretary of Energy

*Secretary of Education
*Secretary of Veterans Affairs
*Secretary of Homeland Security

At this point in the chapter we have covered the important stuff about the job of President, but before we end it, there are a few small bits of "Awesome" that come along with the job that haven't been mentioned yet . . .

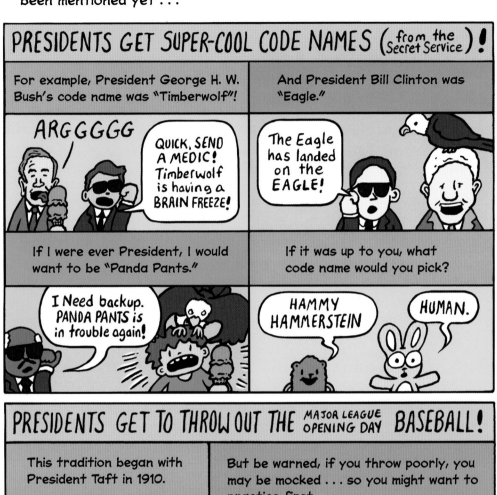

PRESIDENTS CAN GET STUFF NAMED AFTER THEM!

Some Examples

| SCHOOLS | AIRPORTS | STUFFED TOY BEARS |

LINCOLN Elementary

JFK AIRPORT

Teddy's BEAR

When President Theodore Roosevelt (nicknamed Teddy) was on a hunting trip, he refused to shoot a bear that was chained up. The news of his good sportsmanship spread and soon after, stuffed bears were being made and sold as Teddy's bears . . .

PRESIDENTS GET TO BE CARTOONS !!!!

When you are a President you will be drawn as a cartoon by a lot of political cartoonists . . .

I don't think this looks like me at all!

It may not always be flattering, but you are a cartoon, and that is AWESOME!!!

Last Awesome bit of this chapter: PRESIDENTS GET A PAYCHECK!

Presidents have a tough job, but they do get paid . . . the current amount is $400,000 a year plus a bunch of perks.

Of course, earning a good paycheck is not the best reason to run for President...

FREE HOUSING

Lots of secret friends

Air Force one

AND MORE ...

Then what is?

That's a good question . . .

Clearly, the question "What are good reasons to run for President?" is a good one . . . And since cute animals easily get distracted by milk shakes, perhaps you (the reader) should answer this question yourself. Go ahead, make a list, give it a try . . .

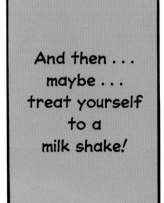

Chapter 6

What Happens When Presidents Are No Longer President?

This chapter takes a look at what retirement is like for Presidents . . .

In previous chapters, we have learned that the Constitution gives the President all sorts of important responsibilities...

responsibilities often = lots of paperwork

SIGH

Plus, we also learned of a few ceremonial duties that tradition gave us, such as the pardoning of the Thanksgiving turkey.

YOU'RE FREE, TURKEY! FREE!

THAT WAS NICE... BUT NOW WHAT'S FOR DINNER?

UMM...

THAT WASN'T A TURKEY, THAT WAS THE VICE PRESIDENT'S WIFE...

EEEEP

But there's one thing we haven't learned yet, and that's "What does a President do when the job is eventually over?"

I HAVE NO CLUE...

Well, I think it's obvious... the next thing you do is run for President of the Milky Way Galaxy!

UMM... you have a beautiful baby. Vote for me!

Sorry, bunny. No such job exists and before you say it, neither does the job as "Unicorn Hunter."

Sigh...

128

The fact is, assuming you are not killed in office by an assassin . . .
Like these four Presidents were . . .

And as long as you don't die in office like these four
Presidents did . . .

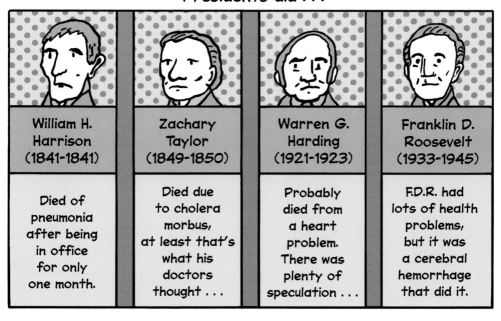

A retired President can do whatever he or she wants to do . . .
assuming it's not illegal . . .

Some Presidents have gone on to do some exciting things upon leaving the office. For example, ex-President Theodore Roosevelt (1901-1909) went on a spectacular African safari/hunting trip . . .

President George H. W. Bush (1989-1993) has gone skydiving several times since leaving the job . . .

George at 85

Many ex-Presidents remain politically active in one way or another . . .

I endorse this candidate.

I do not endorse this bunny... for anything.

It probably isn't surprising that some former Presidents remain involved with politics, but what may be surprising is that some former Presidents continue to seek political offices for themselves.

SOME EXAMPLES

John Quincy Adams went from being President (1825-1829)	Andrew Johnson went from being President (1865-1869)	And William Howard Taft went from being President (1909-1913)
		Nice mustache!
to winning a seat on the House of Representatives . . .	to becoming a senator . . .	to being Chief Justice of the Supreme Court.
		THANKS, YOU TOO!

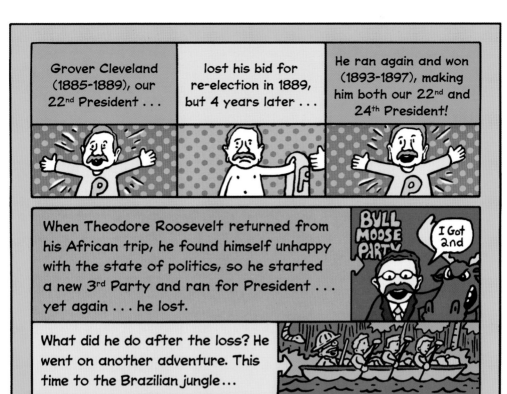

Grover Cleveland (1885-1889), our 22nd President . . .

lost his bid for re-election in 1889, but 4 years later . . .

He ran again and won (1893-1897), making him both our 22nd and 24th President!

When Theodore Roosevelt returned from his African trip, he found himself unhappy with the state of politics, so he started a new 3rd Party and ran for President . . . yet again . . . he lost.

BULL MOOSE PARTY

I Got 2nd

What did he do after the loss? He went on another adventure. This time to the Brazilian jungle . . .

Two former Presidents got to see their own kids become Presidents . . .	George H. W. Bush	George W. Bush	John Adams	John Quincy Adams
	Dad (1989-1993)	Son (2001-2009)	Dad (1797-1801)	Son (1825-1829)

Some ex-Presidents make it a point to completely slip away from public life upon leaving the office . . .

SOME EXAMPLES . . .

censored

censored

censored

The above panels have been censored to respect their privacy desires . . .

Since a lot of exciting and important stuff can happen while one is President, it should not be surprising that ex-Presidents will spend a lot of time reflecting on the experience . . .

Here are a few examples of former President Calvin Coolidge reflecting.

Coolidge thinking.

BEEP BEEP BEEP CRASH ! Hee Hee Hee

Coolidge discussing.

Hey Billy, remember how I used to push those buttons?

Coolidge reading.

HOW CALVIN PUSHED MY BUTTONS

Gee... He did not have a sense of humor.

I need to tell the real story of my presidency!

Some ex-Presidents even write down their reflections on their presidency.

Finished...

The results are called "Presidential Memoirs."

THE Autobiography of Calvin Coolidge

In recent times, presidential memoirs have become commonplace. (Now it's almost expected of former Presidents . . .)

A few recent examples:

Ex-President Ronald Reagan (1981-1989)

Ex-President George H. W. Bush (1989-1993)

Ex-President Bill Clinton (1993-2001)

Ex-President George W. Bush (2001-2009)

But presidential memoirs were not as common in America's early days . . . The first one wasn't published until 1866.

It was by our 15th President, James Buchanan (1857-1861)

It was called . . .

Mr. Buchanan's Administration on the Eve of Rebellion

These days nobody really remembers that our 15th President wrote a memoir, but the same can't be said of our 18th President.

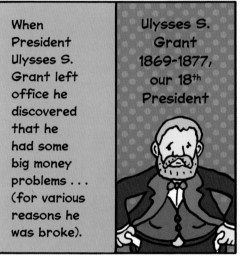

When President Ulysses S. Grant left office he discovered that he had some big money problems . . . (for various reasons he was broke).

Ulysses S. Grant 1869-1877, our 18th President

His friend Mark Twain (a famous writer) offered Grant a lucrative contract to publish his memoir. Grant couldn't say no . . .

Mark Twain

Author of *The Adventures of Tom Sawyer* and lots more.

Grant wrote his memoir and it became a huge success!

Sadly, Grant died before he could see the money rain in.

At least his widow would not be left poor.

SOB SOB

YAY!

SOB SOB SOB

Grant proved (without trying) that a presidential memoir could be interesting, informative, and still be remembered years later (not to mention that it could make a lot of money).

After President Grant, presidential memoirs became much more frequent.

If I am ever President I would write a large part of my memoirs in comic format. Plus, I would make it waterproof, so it could be read in a bathtub!!!

134

Another way former Presidents can make money is by giving speeches!

Sometimes, organizations (like colleges and businesses) will pay ex-Presidents to come and give talks or speeches . . .

THEN I SAID, "LEAVE ME ALONE, PANCAKE MONSTER! YOU'RE GETTING SYRUP ON ME."

Most likely the organizations want speeches that are inspirational, and pertain to your presidency, not just a detailed retelling of your very strange dreams.

Oh...

Plus, if they wanted, they could probably make money doing product endorsements!

Product

BROWN GRAINY Fiber-O's

MMM Yummy

Product

BABY Deodorizers

MAKE STINKY BABIES A THING OF THE PAST!

Perhaps, to prevent broke ex-Presidents from being forced to peddle "Brown Grainy Fiber O's," Congress passed the Former Presidents Act (F.P.A.) in 1958 . . .

The new law provided former Presidents an annual pension.

Currently it is . . .

$191,300

Plus, there are a bunch of other perks in the Act as well, such as . . .

Money for travel . . .

Money for office stuff and a staff . . .

And continued Secret Service protection is provided . . .

Pre-1997 ex-Presidents get protection for life, after 1997 they get Secret Service protection for 10 years.

Now we will cover a problem many ex-Presidents faced . . .

What to do with all the official documents and personal papers that amass during one's Presidency?

WHERE DO WE GO?   NOBODY KNOWS.

Over the years some Presidents saved their records, but often they were poorly stored or taken care of.

munch munch

MMMM History is Yummy.

Many records were just lost.

We're not lost... We're here...

Yeah, you're lost

Lots of presidential papers were divided up and are now in a zillion different places.

And a few Presidents (like Chester A. Arthur) destroyed all their papers.

HA HA HA YOU'RE FREE!

When President Franklin D. Roosevelt was faced with the document problem, he decided to build a library specifically to keep his papers safe, in one place, and easily accessible for future generations. He even included lots of other personal things in the library, making it a museum of sorts.

President F.D.R.

(1933-1945)

F.D.R.'s library, located on his home estate in N.Y.

Although this chapter is focused on Presidents after the presidency, it should be noted that F.D.R. built his library while still a President . . .

Both the Presidents before and after Franklin D. Roosevelt must have liked his solution, because they built their own presidential libraries too . . . (only unlike F.D.R. they did it after their presidencies).

Thus a tradition had been set, and every President since has built a library in his home state with privately raised funds . . . "Each is special in its own way," said the mommy library.

Once built, the libraries are turned over to the care of the National Archives and Records Administration (N.A.R.A. for short). Other libraries (of pre-Hoover Presidents) have been built since, but they are not taken care of by N.A.R.A.

*Another quick note from the author

If I were ever President I would make my library a giant treehouse filled with smart monkey assistants to help historians and researchers.

And now a quick question from the author to you, the reader.

Do you live near a presidential library?

Because if you do, you should check it out. They are filled with cool stuff (in addition to documents).

But somehow, many ex-Presidents still find time to do charity work. Below are a few examples . . .

Former President Carter liked to do volunteer work with a charity called Habitat for Humanity.

Habitat builds affordable homes for those in need by using volunteer labor and donations.

Carter's fame brought the charity . . .

a lot of good attention, helping them grow.

In 2004, when a huge tsunami (a giant wave) caused massive damage in South Asia, the President (at the time) George W. Bush asked the two most recent Presidents to head a campaign to raise private funds to help.

George H. W. Bush   Bill Clinton

The American people responded generously . . .

In 2010, when a devastating earthquake hit Haiti, once again, the current President (Barack Obama) asked the two most recent Presidents to head a campaign to raise funds to help.

Bill Clinton   George W. Bush

Once again, the American people responded generously.

As this short chapter comes to a close, if there's one thing you should have learned, it's that when a President is done being President, his or her life doesn't just end. In many cases it is only beginning.

At least until you die!

Nice reminder, bunny. And speaking of death, let's end this chapter with an interesting former-President death factoid!

YAY!

The interesting factoid: 3 ex-Presidents have died on July 4th!

John Adams	Thomas Jefferson	James Monroe

And now a closing warning: The overuse of interesting factoids can be considered very annoying . . .

HAPPY 4th of July, FRIEND!

THANKS, AND A HAPPY ANNIVERSARY OF THE DEATHS OF JEFFERSON, ADAMS, AND MONROE, TO YOU, FRIEND.

Umm...WOULD YOU LIKE A HOT DOG OR A HAMBURGER OR BOTH?

I'LL HAVE BOTH, AND SPEAKING OF BOTH, DID YOU KNOW THAT BOTH THOMAS JEFFERSON AND JOHN ADAMS DIED ON THE SAME JULY 4th in 1826 (EXACTLY 50 years after the first one)?

NO...

I DID NOT KNOW THAT.

SPEAKING OF NOT KNOWING, JOHN ADAMS DID NOT KNOW THAT JEFFERSON HAD DIED RIGHT BEFORE HIM, BECAUSE HIS LAST WORDS WERE "JEFFERSON SURVIVES"!!!

I'M ANNOYING YOU, AREN'T I? yup

We warned you.

THE END

THE CONCLUSION

As this book is about to come to an END . . .

You (the reader) may have noticed that you have absorbed a lot of wonderful presidential information . . .

Before reading the book

HMMM

and

Knowledge Hurts

after reading the book.

You learned things like . . .

How the job of President was created (and how it wasn't) . . .

President-us Appear-us Now-us!

POOF

How the presidential election process works . . .

VOTE FOR

SAL

I AM NOT A ROBOT! And I want to kiss your babies!

Where the President lives and works . . . and bowls . . .

SMASH

STRIKE!

And you learned a lot about the different aspects of the actual job (including the paperwork).

MR. PRESIDENT! WE WANT YOU TO BUILD US A LIBRARY!

NOT NOW, GUYS

BUT MR. PRESIDENT...

I SAID NOT NOW... WE'LL DEAL WITH IT WHEN I RETIRE!

In this book you also learned about some of the bad aspects of the job.

Like how the President needs constant protection.

THE CHICKEN IS SAFE IN HIS COOP!

HEY, I THOUGHT WE AGREED MY CODE NAME WOULD BE DOCTOR DANGER?

NOPE, WE DID NOT AGREE ON THAT!

And how Presidents are very busy and get very little privacy . . .

MR. PRESIDENT, I NEED YOUR SIGNATURE ON THESE...

MR. PRESIDENT, I HAVE 20 PEOPLE WAITING TO SPEAK WITH YOU AT YOUR OFFICE.

MR. PRESIDENT WOULD YOU PLEASE ADOPT ME?

ARGGG!

Plus, the fact that embarrassing stuff does not stay hidden.

EXTRA EXTRA READ ALL ABOUT IT!

PRESIDENT SCARED OF CATS

THE PRESIDENT IS AFRAID OF KITTENS

MR. PRESIDENT, IS WHAT THEY'RE SAYING TRUE?

SADLY YES

Then don't look down!

Huh

Clearly, there is a lot more that could be learned, in addition to what's in this book, but there's good news . . . You can't be President until you are at least 35. This means that you have . . .

For example, think about all the things that George Washington did before he became President . . .

He studied hard to learn good manners . . . (and other stuff)

He worked as a surveyor . . .

He obtained a military position and played a part in the French and Indian War . . .

He was married and began a life as a farmer.

SMOOOOOCH

He got involved in politics and grew annoyed with Great Britain's growing tyranny . . .

Grrrr!

He accepted the job as commander in chief of the newly created Continental Army . . .

And he eventually led the United States to victory.

YAY YAY YAY

He then returned to the farm . . .

And it was thanks to all these experiences that he became the man the people elected: a respected, responsible, freedom-loving, humble, patriotic leader! So, if you want to be President there is no rush . . . You have time . . . but you may want to continue learning about the history of America, and perhaps start reading up on the lives of individual Presidents and the experiences that made them who they were.

So, go get some books and start reading!!!

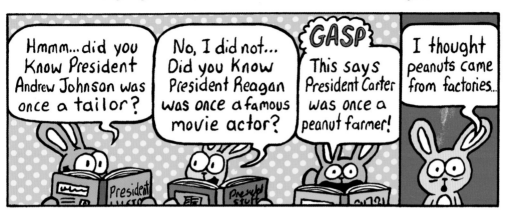

Another great way to learn history is by watching documentaries!

And maybe you can convince your parents to take you to visit a presidential museum or some other American historic park/museum!

You may think this drawing is over-the-top, but you will never know until you check one out . . .

One last note to all the bunnies out there . . .

Some After-Content Content

The following bonus pages contain silly cartoon drawings of the first 44 Presidents of the United States...

Riding ON DINOSAURS!

152

Bibliography

Batchelder, Drew. (2009) *Teddy Bears and Peanut Soup: Presidential Trivia.* Hammond.

Bennett, William J. (2006) *America: The Last Best Hope Volume I: From the Age of Discovery to a World at War.* Nashville, TN: Thomas Nelson.

———. (2007) *America: The Last Best Hope Volume II: From a World at War to the Triumph of Freedom.* Nashville, TN: Thomas Nelson.

Chernow, Ron. (2011 paperback edition) *Washington: A Life.* New York, NY: Penguin Group (USA) Inc.

Davis, Kenneth C. (2001) *Don't Know Much About the Presidents:* HarperCollins.

Ellis, Joseph J. (2002 paperback edition). *Founding Brothers.* First Vintage Books Edition.

———. (2008 paperback edition). *American Creation.* First Vintage Books Edition.

Kelly, C. Brian. (2005 edition). Best Little Stories From the White House (2nd Edition). Nashville, TN: Cumberland House Publishing.

Lansford, Tom, ed. (2007) *The Presidential Election Process* (Opposing Viewpoint series). Greenhaven Press.

McCullough, David G. (2006 paperback edition) 1776. New York, NY: Simon & Schuster.

Schweikart, Larry and Michael Allen. (2007 paperback edition). *A Patriot's History of the United States.* New York, NY: Sentinel (Penguin Group (USA) Inc.)

WEBSITES:

www.whitehouse.gov

www.whitehousemuseum.org

www.whitehousehistory.org

www.presidentialpetmuseum.com

www.senate.gov/index.htm

www.archives.gov

people.howstuffworks.com/presidential-memoir.htm

www.secretservice.gov